ROSEMARY HAWTHORNE describes herself in these words, "I answer to the name of wife, housewife, clergy-wife, and Mum × 7. Ex-actress, do-it-yourself upholsterer, rotten cook, good at sewing, dog lover, and middle-aged, I am at my happiest sorting through a trunk of old, old dresses."

As a former actress who studied at the Royal Academy of Dramatic Art, Rosemary has developed a keen eye for the way people dress. "To observe clothes is to observe society," she says. Her modelled shows, *Two Hundred Years of Fashion*, draw crowded audiences, many charities benefiting as a result. Her success is due as much to her witty and knowledge-able commentary as to the skill of her presentation.

MARY WANT, art school student with a passionate interest in costume and fashion, began her career in an advertising agency and then worked free-lance as a commercial artist, specialising in calligraphy. Married, with two grown-up children, she devotes herself to painting water-colours of Romney Marshes when she is not helping to run an enchanting smallholding.

Some years ago she went to one of Rosemary's fashion shows and amused herself by sketching the dresses displayed. Rosemary saw her work and vowed that the two would collaborate when she started to write. OH . . . KNICKERS! is the first fruit of this partnership.

OH . . . KNICKERS!

A BRIEF HISTORY OF "UNMENTIONABLES"

OH . . . KNICKERS!

A BRIEF HISTORY OF "UNMENTIONABLES"

by

Rosemary Hawthorne

Drawings by

Mary Want

BACHMAN & TURNER
London

OH . . . KNICKERS!

A brief history of ''unmentionables''

First published in the United Kingdom in 1985 by
BACHMAN & TURNER
9 Cork Street
Mayfair
London WIX 1PD

ISBN 0 85974 129X (Limp)
     0 85974 133 8 (Cloth)

Typeset in Univers by PGH Typesetting, Maidstone
Printed and bound in Great Britain by Headley Brothers Ltd.
Book design and production by Highmonde Ltd.

This book is dedicated to my three daughters, Samantha, Arabella and Phoebe Alice — who know a lot about knickers.

''Dress and sin came in together, and have kept good
fellowship ever since.''
The Habits of Good Society (c 1858)

INTRODUCTION

This book is intended as a small entertainment. I set down these intimate details as a mark of profound respect for the most basic of female garments.

The history is not long — barely two hundred years — which is nothing much compared with other dress history of the civilised world. But in that time it has had a distinct rise and fall, and has seen womankind through thick and thin.

Our English female ancestors in the early centuries cared not one jot about covering their lower parts with a separate item of clothing. Lengthy skirts, which had an abundance of material, a petticoat and a long linen shift or chemise worn against the skin was all the protection thought necessary — or, indeed, healthy. An eighteenth century woman of fashion was concerned with what was worn and seen on the outside — and that was all. All her effort — and that of her maid — went into producing a public effect. The steel busked, whale-bone corset, the hooped petticoat or false rump were all endured for the sake of her fashionably-silked outside appearance. She was a child of nature in private matters — quite in accordance with the rumbustious, earthy manners of her time.

But at the close of the eighteenth century — when revolution had torn France apart, and war had raged on each side of the English Channel — women began to reveal more of themselves on the outside — the dresses became soft, clinging, sensuously transparent — India muslins were the "in" materials — and, for the first time, women felt exposed enough to need another undergarment. Perhaps it was the dawning awareness of their sexuality and what a valuable commodity it could prove; perhaps it was an unconscious attempt to remove the blatant excesses of their mothers and grandmothers; or perhaps it was that these fine cotton dresses were just plain chilly — whatever — here life really begins for the Gemini of the closet.

The first pair of 'drawers' on the scene — in the early 1800's — are reported to have been "light pink" — flesh coloured. Divided, separate legs that attached to a waistband and laced at the back, they could be knee-length or to the ankle. When ankle-length, they were first called pantaloons and later pantalettes. As the century progressed, this term was used only with regard to children's wear.

Drawers were cut on somewhat masculine lines, for it seems only fair to point out that men had known the discreet luxury of underpants since the sixteenth century, which only goes to prove what women have long suspected: that men keep the best ideas to themselves as long as possible!

By about 1820, it could be said that drawers were part of the daily wear of duchesses — and a few others — but it was to take a good dose of Victorian prudery to urge the uninclined masses into these new-fangled garments. Victoria succeeded to the throne in 1837, and her long reign eventually enveloped women in veritable snowdrifts of virgin cambric and calico. The Victorians, filled as always with a great pioneering zeal, boldly sought to structure the Great British Knicker. The Regency was only playing at it — it took the all-conquering, Empire-building, morally self-righteous Victorians to raise true blue-bagged, starched linen to undreamed-of heights — and depths.

This is a social account, touching on women of every class. It is a charming, lively, interesting and, often, amusing story taking Women's Suffrage, two World Wars and Government Restrictions in its stride.

No other item of dress has suffered such mixed reactions. It produces a range of emotion from pink-cheeked embarrassment and coy giggles to downright dirty-minded guffaws. No other piece of human adornment has been subject to so much ambiguous association . . . in satin and lace, they are the acceptable, intimate gift of a lover; in bottle green, grey or navy blue Botany yarn, the much hated part of schoolgirl uniform; and in snatches of Lurex, marabou-trimmed, the saucy token of promiscuous sex.

Here is their story . . .

"... AND WHAT DID *YOU* CALL THEM, MUMMY?"

No other garment has ever been called such a bewildering variety of names over the years. These, I suspect, are only some of them . . .

Breeches, Trowsers, Pantaloons, Pantalettes, Drawers, Knickerbockers, Knickers (Knicks), Small Clothes (Smalls), Indescribables, Unmentionables, Bloomers, Bockers, Nether Garments, French Knickers, Divided Skirts, Step-in's, Camiknickers (Teddies), Combinations (Combs.), Pants, Panties, Pantees, Briefs, Passion Killers, Scanties . . . and YOU, dear reader, will possibly know one or two more!

Lines written by an Admirer to commemorate . . .

MISS PEARSON'S PLAIN PROPERTY

These Drawers are plain
(Quite unlike thee . . .)
The needlework is fine.
Oh, Virgin Stuff that has most right
To clasp those limbs sublime!
Would I could dolly, starch and iron —
Thus serve this pair divine —
For, dear Miss Pearson, I perceive
These longcloth legs are thine.

Miss Pearson was the original owner of these 1840's drawers

Longcloth drawers
with braces.
1843

detail of knitted lace

THE GREAT EXHIBITION

There is a certain gaunt splendour about these fine drawers. Called "drawers" because they "drew on", the completely separate legs measure forty inches from the top of the waistband to the modestly embroidered and tucked trim at the foot. In general, early undergarments such as these have little in the way of embellishment, as though even the thought of enticing prettiness would besmirch the wearer. Purity in thought and thread! These cotton poplin drawers are entirely handsewn, with very neat little stitches, and tie around the waist with wide tapes.

The date, marked on the waistband in india ink, is 1851 — the year of Prince Albert's — Queen Victoria's consort — most renowned venture: the Great Exhibition; also marked is "No. 4", the set number, as it was usual for underclothes to be made in sets of a dozen. A sewing maid might have worked these . . . and would have earned about one shilling a pair.

Over the drawers would have been worn a gathering multitude of petticoats to cope with the ever-expanding skirts. Drawers of this pattern continued to be worn for nigh on the next twenty years — peeping coyly from under the swaying, metal-banded crinoline cage — invented in 1856 — until the collapse of such edifices by the late 1860s. It can be fairly accurately assumed that even then there were many older women who preferred and wore these "long legs" up to the close of the century.

It was considered indelicate in any way to allude to ladies' legs; they were creatures with poetic "limbs". Women were supposed to "float" over the ground.

L. O. Acres.
No 4. 1851.
Cotton
poplin
drawers
1851
detail of
embroidery

We can only imagine the intoxicating effect it must have had on a man to catch sight of these bewitching white trousers, artfully darting beneath the voluminous skirt. This was, doubtless, part of the Victorian female's mantrap — "now you see, now you don't"! Propriety — and passion — in its proper place.

No wonder some women chose to wear them for a lifetime: at a shilling a pair they were cheap at the price.

BARELY CONCEALED

Lady Chesterfield writes a letter to her daughter, c. 1850:

". . . skirts that ended one inch above my ancles showing the vandyked or frilled edges of those comfortable garments which we have borrowed from the other sex, and which all of us wear but none of us talk about . . ."

A. BLOOMER . . . REFORMER

It so happens that in 1851 — by strange coincidence — an American woman, Mrs. Amelia Jenks Bloomer, an ardent campaigner for Women's Rights, with Healthier Dressing as part of her manifesto, travelled to London and Dublin to speak on Reform Dress and the Demon Drink.

She was not well received, and her appearances were greeted with ridicule. She wore a hip-length coat and the long Turkish-style trousers, baggy and gathered at the ankle, that have become synonymous with her name.

Ironically, she did not design this outfit — it was the idea of her friend and fellow campaigner, a British woman named Elizabeth Miller. But "Millers" doesn't have quite the same mirth-making ring to it — I can understand why it didn't catch on!

Mrs Bloomer
1851

A MISS ADVENTURE

From Lord Cowley's "Memoirs" 1855:
"Despatch from our Ambassador in Paris on the visit of King Victor Emmanuel. Lord Cowley reports that at a state reception a Lady in Waiting had the misfortune to trip over her crinoline skirt and tumble headlong in view of the Imperial party, whereupon the King exclaimed with enthusiasm to the Empress, 'I am delighted to see, Madam, that your ladies do not wear les calecons, and that the Gates of Paradise are always open!' "

A Miss-Adventure

UNSEEN AMIDST THE WINTER SNOW

One thing is certain: a crinoline cage must have been a trifle draughty for winter wear.

These are a very substantial pair of open-legged drawers. Measuring thirty-three inches in length and thirty-nine inches around the waist! They are made of a lovely warm material called angola (a mixture of cotton and llama goat wool). They have a fleecy appearance on the inside, and must have been a great comfort during inclement weather. It is possible that a fine pair of cotton drawers might have been worn over them.

The date is approximately 1865 — they are machine-stitched and hand-finished. The lock stitch sewing machine was in use by dressmakers in the 1850s — one of the most revolutionary inventions of Victorian domestic life.

Amusing though it is to think of the rotund matron who first wore these winsome warmers, they were probably a practical necessity when making a journey in a horsedrawn carriage through the winter snows. Apart from that, Victorian houses were not known for over-heating . . . nor even palaces . . . since, would you believe, these snug claddings once belonged to a French princess! (Propriety forbids mentioning her name, but her size and shape seem to have rivalled Victoria herself.)

TEENY BOTTOMS

A pair of doll's drawers, measuring twelve inches, handsewn. Small copies of the prevailing fashion of the mid-nineteenth century.

Fleecy
winter drawers
1865

Doll's drawers
1860-70

ONCE MORE UNTO THE BREACH . . .

By the late 1870s, drawers, now generally worn by all classes of women, became shorter and narrower in cut. The fashionable bustle dress of the 1870s and 1880s required smooth lines over the hips and thighs. The interest was now heavily concentrated at the back of the skirt, with great loops and puffs of material. The front of the skirt was slim, sheath-like, the back being caught on the inside with tying tapes.

This pair of crisp white cotton, machine-stitched drawers measure thirty inches long. They button at the centre back and are more like breeches in appearance, though the frill of lace gives them femininity.

The sewing machine brought new freedom to women — clothes could be made quickly — therefore there were more clothes available — and trimming was easily applied. Imagine a world where every single item of clothing had to be handmade.

These were the years of transition in women's lives. The first Women's Suffrage Committee was formed in 1866 — and by the 1870s many, many women were involved with the cause. Physical education was pleaded for in girls' schools, and in the 1880s there was the first "health cult". Viscountess Harberton led a group of convinced Society women into forming the Rational Dress Society (shades of Mrs. Bloomer). This was in 1881 and in the following year a Hygienic Wearing Apparel Exhibition was held in Kensington Town Hall.

"A Healthy Mind in a Healthy Body" was the new rallying cry of the decade. Aertex cotton was invented and put into production. Many manufacturers advertised chamois leather underclothes for

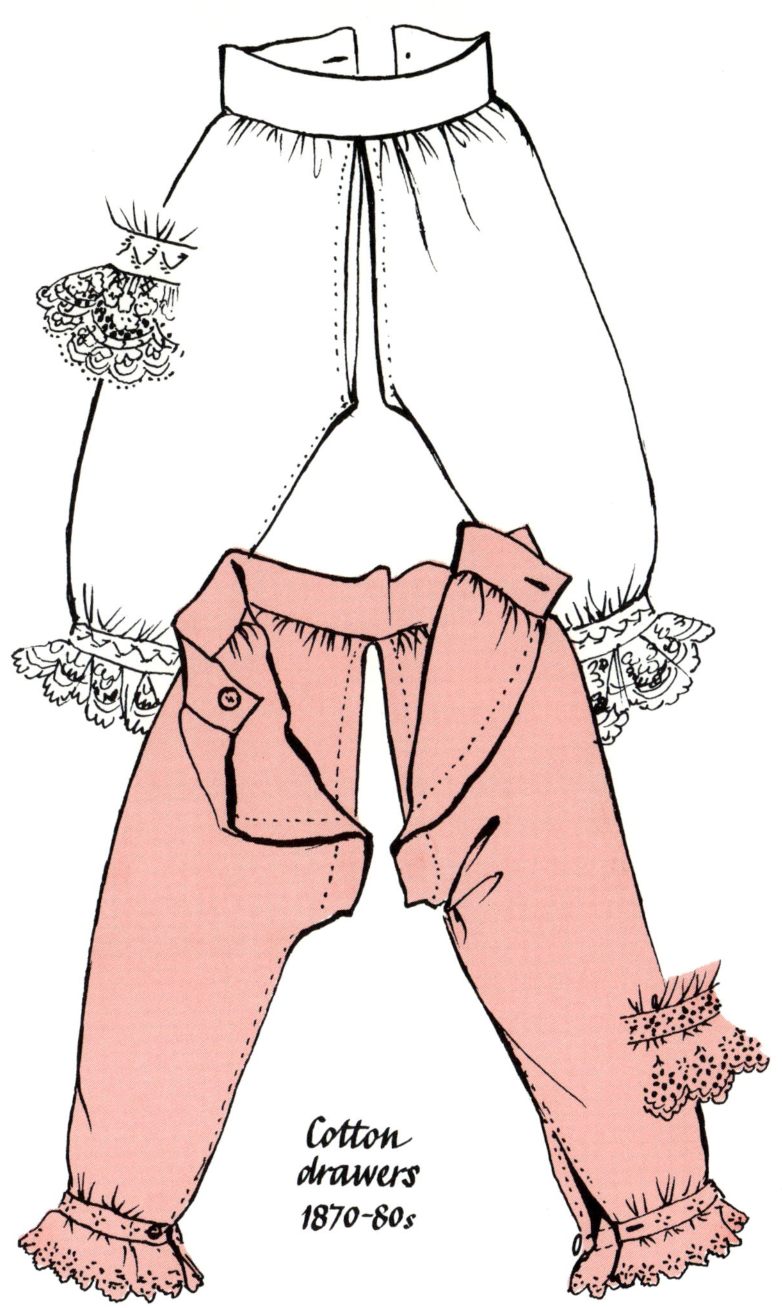

Cotton
drawers
1870-80s

"everyday wear". Can you think of anything nastier?
But, Dr. Gustave Jaeger, introducing his "Sanitary
Woollen System" during the 1870s, advocated one
hundred per cent wool as a second skin. "Wear
nothing else next to the skin."

"Think Wool" certainly worked for the enterprising
German doctor, whose natural, undyed, creamy
grey, woollen clothes won a Gold Medal at "The
Healtheries", an international health exhibition in
1884. An early convert to the "woollener" movement
was an Englishman, Lewis Tomalin. Obtaining the
sole agency for Dr. Jaeger's garments, he and two
cousins founded the famous Jaeger Company in
London.

Regretfully, I have, to date, no pair of "Sanitary"
grey wool Dr. J's in the Collection; perhaps they all
ended up as polishing rags — or stuffing for teddy
bears?

But, instead — irrationally — another pair of open-
legged drawers, again about 1875—1885, this time
buttoning at waist and leg. They are completely
handsewn, but nothing professional about it, rather
an uneven needle, and could have been done by a
child. These are made of heavy cotton (longcloth)
and are "dipped" pale pink, probably at a later date.
They measure thirty-seven inches from the waist to
the frill.

BEWARE . . . HERE DANGER LURKS

From the time of the expanding skirt — the 1850s and 1860s — now supported by the crinoline cage — drawers took on a new significance. There was a sudden fashion for coloured "underneaths". Colour flashed — purple, scarlet and even tartan drawers and "knickerbockers" (that fastened at the knee). Stockings too were often strong colours, and stripes were most popular.

This colourful state was to last for some years, and even in the 1880s scarlet flannel was a hot favourite for winter wear.

Over the page a pair of red flannel open drawers of about 1875–80. They are machined and, not very well, handsewn — very homely articles indeed. They fasten with buttons at the back, and look as though they may have been altered on several occasions. However, they must have been loved for their heat-giving qualities in the depths of January.

They measure thirty inches long, and come complete with moth holes!

After all the years of milk-white undies, these scarlet legs must have caused quite a sensation . . . a psychological "playing with fire" . . .

The early nineteenth century writer, Washington Irving, created a nom de plume: "Diedrich Knickerbocker", a fictitious character in his "History of New York' (1809). The family Knickerbocker were of Dutch extraction, and Cruickshank's illustrations in the book show a style of loose knee-breeches, strapped or tied at the knee. Thus "knickerbockers" became fashionable from the 1860s — worn by men on sporting, casual occasions and by women —

their crinolines — for warmth, comfort, and by healthy types who were "fond of rock-climbing or gardening".

ANOTHER MISS ADVENTURE ?? . . .

In 1859, the Honourable Eleanor Stanley, Lady in Waiting to Queen Victoria, writes.

"I hear that the last new 'fast' ladies' fashion is said to be in wearing 'knickerbockers'"; and she describes how the Duchess of Manchester, during a paper chase, getting too hastily over a stile, "caught a hoop of her cage in it and went regularly head over heels, lighting on her feet with her cage and whole petticoats remaining above her head. They say that there was never such a thing to be seen — and the other ladies hardly knew whether to be thankful or not that a part of her underclothing consisted in a pair of scarlet tartan knickerbockers (the things Charlie shoots in) which were revealed to the view of all the world in general and the Duc de Malakoff in particular". The comment afterwards of that person, "Ma chère, c'était diabolique!" seems fairly apt.

Red flannel drawers

*... another
Miss Adventure*

AN OUTSIZE CHARMER

I think these capacious knickers — that word at last — are one of the delights of the entire Collection. They have enormous character. There is something so generous, nay ample, about their cut and style that I feel the original, handsomely curved, lady who drew them on must have been a bit of a character too.

"Closed" knickers like these came into fashion during the 1880s. Knickers, of course, came out of "Knickerbockers".

This superb pair, very finely handsewn in best quality cambric, with closely worked pin tucks and a buttonhole-stitched edging, measure twenty-nine inches from the top to the knee, while the waist is an abundant thirty-five inches! Three yards of thirty-six inch material were needed to complete these nifty knicks.

However, I am led to believe by the excellence of the sewing that this lady, this cuddly armful, was in the process of putting by her "bottom drawer" — this is a trousseau undie if ever I saw one! Her initials are embroidered neatly in the centre of the garment.

The knickers fasten with the new side-placket buttoning, but still have tapes to pull tightly round and tie. A really trim waist — and I presume in proportion to the rest, thirty-five inches looked trim — was a must in the 1880s, when figure-hugging, nicely fitting, long-line bodices were fashionable.

These admirable knickers blowing on the washing line would make you feel very proud. Small boys might have laughed and called them "rice bags", but the world has forever, mistakenly, called them "Bloomers".

"Closed"
Cambric
knickers.
1885

ANCESTRAL DRAWERS

Not long ago I discovered a pair of white cotton drawers in a Weymouth antique shop: they were made on a Grand Scale — measuring 33 inches long and, at their widest point across the leg, 17 inches. Very roomy!

Entirely handsewn, the back over-laps and fastens with crossing tape ties. The only embellishment is three small tucks at the leg-ends. They date from the late 1850s, early 1860s. The name "E. Wingfield Digby" is clearly marked on a Cash's label; and this presents us with a problem, for the famous Cash's Woven Tape was not manufactured until 1889. On this evidence we can only assume that the lady labelled her linen at a much later date — or wore second-hand drawers. It is a mystery.

The Wingfield Digby family have an "old", respected name historically connected to Dorset. Landowners, church builders and patrons . . .

Come to think of it, a recently retired Archdeacon of Sarum might well be able to shed light on the domestic origins of these quaint, family articles . . .

Cotton
drawers
c. 1860

The Sarum Link

THE NAUGHTY '90s . . . AND THE 'NEW WOMAN'

During the mid-1890s, young women sped forth, the fashionably attired New Women of their generation, perched precariously on their bicycles, dressed in the first obvious take-over from the male wardrobe. This was the serge knickerbocker suit. Women were at last seen to be bipeds! The floating swans had suddenly gained legs.

Bicycling was an absolute mania by the late nineteenth century, and these daring girls, throwing caution to the wind, pedalled like mad — free at last. Their newly discovered freedom was echoed in the "bicycling dress" — a jacket and divided skirt or knickerbockers — often referred to as "rationals": it was the triumphant return of Reform Dress.

Then these jolly Boadiceas seemed to run out of steam — or pedal power — and here are two pairs of really frilly-frillies that seem to be urging the wearers back to a more conventional femininity.

Both pairs of drawers date from the 1890s or early 1900s. Both are beautifully handsewn in fine cotton, have tie tapes at the waist and a good measure of handmade lace to finish them off. The design is still the old "open" style (close rivalry now between open and closed!) and the legs are extremely wide at the knee: twenty-four and twenty-eight inches around. One pair has "squared" points to the frill — a popular feature at the time.

They have all the charm and allurement of the coquette. This was "lingerie" (as distinct from plain underwear). It is fascinating to see that the more women seemed to control their own lives, the more

Fine cotton,
lace-edged
drawers.
1895–1900s.

devastatingly enticing and provocative became their underclothes.

The slang term for open drawers remained, sadly, very brutal: they were referred to as "free traders".

PROFICIENCY TEST

An actress – presumably a bicyclist – sang this delightfully shocking verse in the 1890s;

"Just a little bit of string – such a tiny little thing,
Not as tightly tied as string should be;
So in future when I ride, I shall wear things that divide,
Or things that haven't strings, you see!"

A BLESSED UNION

In 1901, Queen Victoria died, and her self-indulgent, middle-aged son, Edward VII, ascended to the throne. His reign of ten years saw women dressed in some of the most beautiful clothes that ever tempted the daughters of Eve. Perhaps that is as it should be — it was no secret that Edward loved and admired feminine beauty. Women were consciously elegant and well-groomed. The lace, the full-bosomed, high-necked, bloused bodices, the tiny waists, the long trailing skirts trembling with cascades of frills like the wash of a ship and, crowning it all, the confections of milliners' art set onto the mounds of well-coiffured hair. All gave clues to the graceful and pampered lives women led — if they were rich.

The flowing lines of the dresses, following the "cello-shaped" hips, demanded sculptured "underneaths", and exquisite combinations like these were the answer.

Combinations had been introduced at the time of bustle dresses (1870 and 1880). Combinations were the happy marriage between the chemise and the drawers.

The pair overleaf, which I think are quite delightful, are in Mull — a fine, filmy cotton — excellently handsewn and possibly made at a convent. There is a profusion of minute pintucks and lace insertion to be seen, and the garment fastens down the front with linen buttons. The open legs of the combinations are, like the previous frillies, very wide at the flounce. These were part of a set of underclothes made for a wedding trousseau.

This pair has lost its original baby ribbon, which closed the bodice top and tied the fullness at the knee

— so in deference to the year of national mourning for the old Queen, we replaced it with a narrow black ribbon.

This was ten years of luxury. Frou-frou skirts rustling over silk petticoats: a decade of gorgeous, unrepentant seductiveness . . . bringing in its wake the most incredible, far-reaching and conclusive changes for all women.

Very fine cotton
combinations
with lace insertion
1901

ALL GOOD THINGS MUST COME TO AN END . . .

The finest crêpe de Chine, professionally handsewn, finished with a deep frill of Torchon lace and silk bows — tape-tied waist, open-legged drawers — refined and tapered in cut — mark the end of an era: Edward VII died in 1910, and the fashionable world trembled at the first breaths of significant change.

It was to herald the most momentous transitional period in women's lives — it affected the way women lived and therefore what they wore.

Outer clothes became classically slender, and by 1911 the hobble skirt, tightly held at the ankles, became fashion's latest fancy. It was a ridiculous and impractical fashion — psychologically it acted as a brake, a spanner-in-the-works to the inevitable 'freeing' of women that was uppermost in the minds of Mrs. Pankhurst and her kindred spirits. In any event, stride for stride, the hobble skirt could not keep up with the Suffragettes marching steadily on in their plain, functional tailormades, and their sensible underpinnings.

In marked contrast to the silken drawers: a stalwart pair of schoolgirls' knickers — or "rationals" — of 1913. The howls of anguish uttered by teenage schoolgirls over many decades can be sympathetically understood when you see what unattractive garments they were. This is the butt of so many cruel jokes: the much-fabled, commonly derided school "Bloomer"!

Measuring twenty-five inches in length, elasticated at waist and knee (elastic yarn was invented in the nineteenth century — and went on to be improved during the twentieth, but wasn't all that

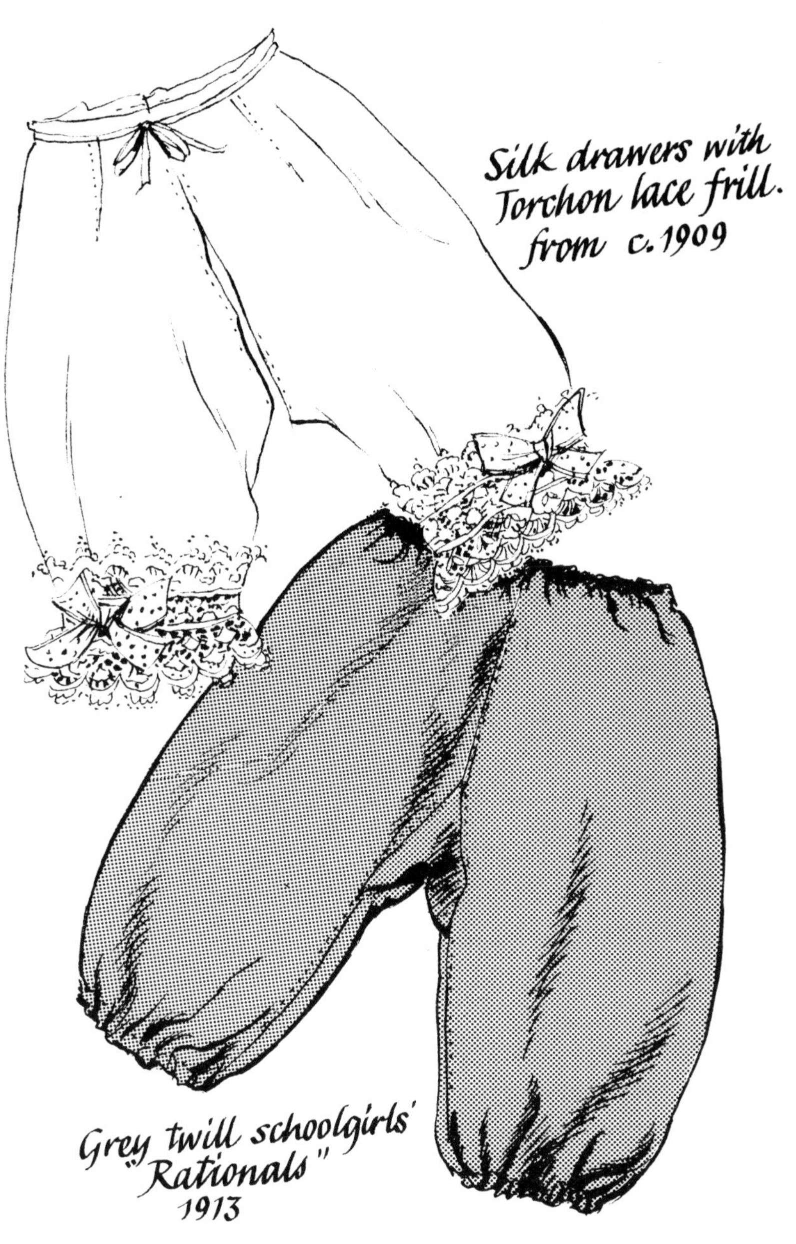

Silk drawers with Torchon lace frill. from c.1909

Grey twill schoolgirls' "Rationals" 1913

"safe" until the 1930s), these "rationals" are made of greyish brown twill, and would have been worn with cotton liners. The knickers represent generations of hot-faced, perspiring young ladies resolutely accepting the disciplines of callisthenics and "honour" on the field.

They are a little bit of English history.

However, these twill-clad legs, released from the miseries of drab school clothes would find fun — and freedom — in the Tango — and, eventually, the Charleston.

GRACEFULLY SEWN

These lovely child's knickers were sent to me by a lady, now in her eighty-fifth year. They were made by her at school in 1914/15.

They are a small triumph of needlework; the stitches so tiny you have to peer to see them. The wide, bowed shape of the knicker is attractive — and fun: I like the "Open Day" label still tacked into place — for these knicks, like all good samples, were for keeping!

Thank you, Grace, for parting with these treasures — I promise them a loving home.

Childs' Knickers made by a schoolgirl
1914 - 15

MOTHER KNEW BEST . . .

A letter written to me early in 1985:

"Dear Mrs. Hawthorne,
    Your unusual hobby reminds me of my Mother. I am a pensioner of 77 and lost my Mother at the age of 88. She was very Victorian in her attitude to me. I was the last of her children after five older brothers.
    Mother was a dress maker and used to make all my clothes. My bloomers, as we would call them, were made of calico cotton, straight down the front, but at the back would be three buttons which I used to have to undo. I have thought since what a very sensible Mother she was because this pattern saved me from a very nasty situation as a child of 6 − which I have never forgotten. My Mother's knickers saved me. But if Mother went to buy any, she used to ask for *Divided Skirts.* I wondered if you had heard knickers referred to as Divided Skirts in the early 1900's.
    I hope I may have given you some interest in Mother's very clever knickers.
    I am no good at drawing but I will try to draw the Knickers I used to wear as a little girl age from 5 to 10.
    Kindest Regards,
    Yours sincerely,
        (Mrs.) O.E.M.
        Chelmsford"

Ten out of ten, Mum!

Child's back-
opening "flap"
combinations.
1910-18

detail

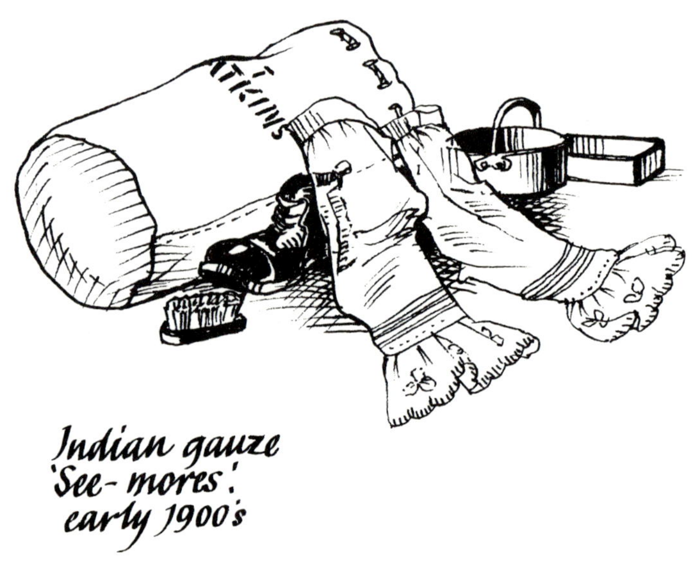

Indian gauze
'See-mores'.
early 1900's

"BRITISH FORCES, FOR THE USE OF . . . SIR"

During the early part of the twentieth century, troops returning to the British Isles after serving long campaigns in India under Lord Seymour brought home these rather ill-made, transparently thin, silk gauze undergarments, as presents for their womenfolk. The drawers were nicknamed "See mores" . . . of course . . .

" . . . THE MONSTROUS REGIMENT OF WOMEN . . . "

The four years of the Great War (1914—18) were radically to alter the conventional, expected role of women. As wives, as mothers, as mistresses, as career women — a good deal was to be lost, but a lot more gained. Some illusions were shattered — but many dreams became realities. The emancipated female had arrived.

As the classes of society slid imperceptibly into different structures, a whole new world inevitably appeared for thousands of women who were formally held within the accepted, centuries-old confines of their male-dominated upbringing. Almost by accident they were shot into a totally new twentieth century. They had, at last, some choice. The ladies' maids turned their back on their mistresses and sought better paid jobs in the munitions factories. Genteel and gently reared young women donned uniforms and joined the V.A.D (Voluntary Aid Detachment), to nurse on the battle-grounds in France. In this country, they rolled up their sleeves and turned their lady-like hands to menial tasks for the War Effort.

Freedom came like glory out of these years. Recognition and the Vote.

The war brought romance and sentiment like all wars. The men away at the front — some girls embroidered their undies with regimental badges. A lot of underwear was still handmade — and the wideleg, frilly, old fashioned open drawers were still in evidence.

These cambric combinations, machine and handsewn, of 1916, show an exuberant amount of embroidery and lace insertion, but the length has shortened, waist to knee, to a mere twenty-one inches. The legs are exceedingly wide — thirty-eight inches around each — but from 1915 the fashion for skirts became fuller, though much shorter, so this amount of material in underwear could be accommodated.

The craze for the Tango had started in 1909 — and it was a most popular dance during the war. These black sarsenet (a fine soft silk) knickers trimmed with silk lace frills are exactly the kind of undie an enthusiastic lady tangoer would have worn — very roomy, allowing plenty of lissom stride — black, and therefore exotic and a bit naughty — like the dance! Paper patterns were printed with instructions on how to "run up" a pair of Tango Knickers.

The success of this dance reflects how society was having to accept a more relaxed attitude towards unchaperoned young women in public. When the men came home on leave they wanted their girls to themselves — and vice versa. Tea Dances were very much in vogue and as much time as possible was spent perfecting the latest steps.

detail of embroidery
Embroidered
cotton
combinations
1914 -18
Black silk and lace
'Tango' knickers

THOSE BRIGHT YOUNG THINGS . . .

After the war, the biggest difference was the reduction in amount of material used to make underclothes. That and their colour.

The chaste white of former decades — slightly chilling in its emotional undertones — was abandoned in favour of a variety of new colours, pink coming out top of the list. Better dyeing processes increased the range of colours — but peach was a favourite shade . . . back to the "flesh pink" of the Regency.

By mid-1920 the skirts shortened to the knee, and the fashionable figure was "boyish". No bosom, no bottom, no curves at all were required — just childlike legs and arms . . . and a long, gracefully set neck: these were the points attributed beautiful by the "fast" social set. The "flappers" twirled their long beads, powdered and painted in public, rouged their knees and kicked up their heels — revealing the minimum of underwear!

These are a pair of camiknickers — the camisole bodice and knickers of yore — in the most delicate of peach-coloured charmeuse (a sensually soft satin) handsewn with a lace trim and three buttons at the crotch; they date from 1925, and were made by a woman undergraduate at Cambridge — she recalls that she felt extremely daring to wear such a liberated garment.

The yellow gauze "ninon" cami — daringly see-me through — has a fairylike vandyked edge and the fragile remains of ribbons that tied between the legs. (I wonder she bothered!)

From the mid 1920s: a pair of cream, crêpe de Chine, directoire knickers. "Directoire" was a style

Crepe de chine knickers
Peach satin cami-knickers
Cream silk camibockers
Pale yellow ninon cami knickers
MADE IN FRANCE for Harrods Ltd LONDON
Pale pink 'Harrods' satin French knickers
1925-30

that was always "closed", and gathered at the knee — the name being revived from the French Directory of the late eighteenth century, when fashionable, racy young women, or "dashers", sported tight knee-breeches under their sheer dresses. This invention of course, crossed the Channel. This pair of knickers have deep panels of ecru lace and bands of satin worked onto them. They are professionally handsewn. Many big stores had "lingerie" departments where articles could be ordered and made bespoke.

A pair of tussore — or washing silk — camibockers of about 1929. These are entirely machine-stitched and fasten with pearl buttons. Camibockers — the teaming of the camisole and erstwhile "knickerbocker" — an undergarment that fastened at the back, providing a "flap" of material that buttoned onto the bodice. Rather complicated and cumbersome as a facility, but a style that was used for children as well . . . the famous Liberty bodice, a kind of soft corset, provided buttons for the knickers in exactly the same way.

The other wide-legged knickers — 1928–1930 — a e called French knickers; the style had at first been fashionable on the Continent. They, too, are in soft pink charmeuse. They have a Harrods' label and are marked as having been "hand made in France". They are professionally and beautifully cut with a side button fastening. They measure eighteen inches in length, and are decorated with the most elegant lace appliqué at the sides.

The slim shape of these beautiful knickers gives a lead to the fashions that were about to emerge in the next ten years.

OPEN MINDED

The old open drawers were not worn much after 1920
— the arrival of the short skirts put paid to them —
but there is a delightful story of a nurse and doctor
examining an old lady during the late 1930s who,
when asked jokingly by the nurse why she continued
to wear these old-fashioned articles, replied, with
some asperity, "I like to air me parts!"

There is no answer to that . . .

A VERY STRONG FEELING OF BIAS . . .

By the 1930s came the vogue for bias cut clothes — cutting material "on the cross" of the grain. Material used like this elongated the figure, accentuating the female body — so that clothes clung revealingly to the contours. Never before had women been so figure-conscious — and dieting became fashionable. Hollywood — and Greta Garbo — were undoubtedly leading influences in this new technique with clothes. The silver screen goddess was very slim, exceedingly elegant, and promoted the fashions that she wore on and off the studio set. It has to be one of the most chic and exquisitely dressed decades.

I think it can be summed up in a sentence reputed to have been spoken by the Duchess of Windsor: "You cannot be too thin — nor too rich!"

Professional tailoring and dressmaking maintained an extremely high standard, and paper patterns, now very good indeed, gave the home dressmaker a chance to show off her skills in a variety of styles.

Camiknickers — sometimes referred to as a "teddy" and French knickers remained very popular. These two French knickers both handsewn and machine-stitched, are made of silk, and bias cut. The very wide legs — often doubling as a petticoat — are decorated by some restrained embroidery.

A pair of very fine silk stockinette or milanese ladies' breeches, c.1930, worn under ski clothes or riding jodhpurs. Marked with the label "Elliot of Hawick" Scotch Underwear. Obviously most warm, comfortable and flexible nether garments.

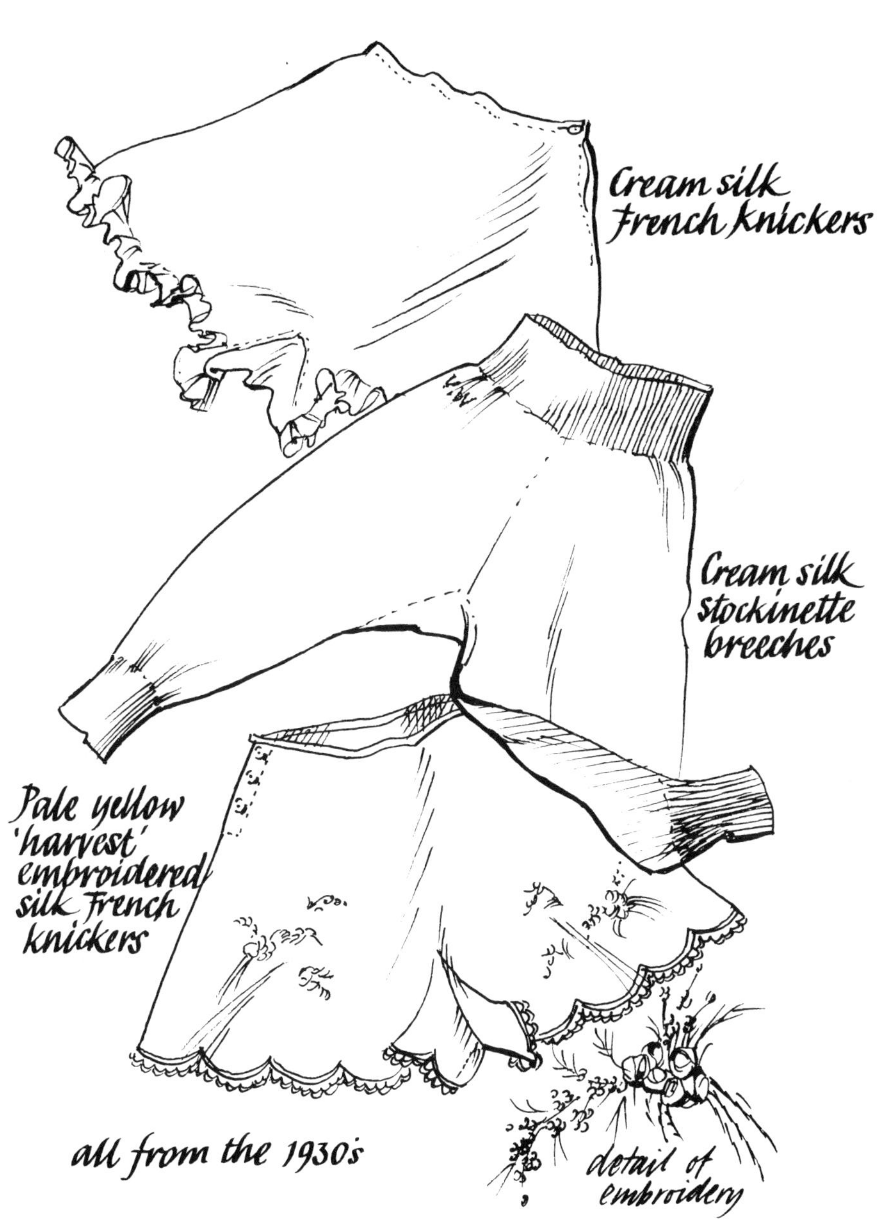

Cream silk
French knickers
Cream silk
stockinette
breeches
Pale yellow
'harvest'
embroidered
silk French
knickers
all from the 1930's
detail of
embroidery

SLOWCOACH FROM CHINA

Just when I thought I was through with knickers —
that, for the purposes of this book — I had handled
my last pair of unmentionables, this pair of
delectables arrived. A girlfriend's mother had been
"turning out" some possessions and had come
across them hidden demurely away, at the back of a
drawer. I found them irresistible — they struck a
romantic chord.

Made in Hong Kong — dated about 1920/25 —
they are, in fact, a very special lace. Cream coloured
net "ground" with fine chiffon appliquéd in an
abstract design, completely oversewn and edged
with cream silk. The front and back have satin heart-
shaped centre panels. These wide, French knickers
are entirely handsewn, with side-button fastenings.

The total effect is very, very pretty and feminine.

Such work reaffirms how unbeatable the Chinese
are when it comes to decorative sewing skills. It is
simply superb.

O.K. — this maid from Hong Kong was VERY late
in arriving — but, since she's a beauty — I'm more
than happy to let her join the party . . .

c. 1920-25 French Knickers
Cream net with chiffon and satin panels.
Made in Hong Kong.

detail of
lace

9th August 1931

Dearest Daphne,

Everything is bliss! The weather, the place, the hotel — Everything!

Most bliss is Reggie. He is too heavenly. This is the luckiest girl in the world!

Daphs, thanks a bundle for being a perfect angel and helping me Get Through! I knew you were a friend to rely on. I thought you looked absolutely sweet — lilac is your colour. Wasn't Venetia's ensemble amazing? (Although I do think you have to be so careful with magenta.)

Mummy forced herself to be bright with simply everyone — but Daddy looked awfully cross — thinking about all the beastly expense, I suppose.

Did you see Pip?? Too much champagne; he was sick all up the stairs and Nanny grumbled most fearfully — said he wasn't her brave soldier any- more — just a stupid one!

What a relief it's all over! I couldn't bear another happy day like that in a lifetime.

Love and kisses,
Prue.

P.S. Reggie, the darling, has just bought me the most divine undies you ever saw. Ravissant! Daphs, the knicks are unbelievable..... positively indecent!! I'll never dare wear them in Esher.

SWEET NOTHINGS

Prue's unbelievables; Two peach-coloured, pleated silk "flaps" with a "hinge" of silk slung between. Side buttoned. A design possibly based on the Ancient Egyptian loincloth called a "schenti". Or . . . "scanty", perhaps?

ARTY CRAFTY

Seeing is believing — or so they say. By 1920 a silk lookalike was on the market. Artificial silk, "Art Silk", was first commercially produced by the American Viscose Company in 1910. It was used to make the new, "soft" collared shirts; later, underclothes were being made from this material. It was not identical to real silk. It was manufactured from various products such as wood pulp, corn protein and chemical compounds. "Rayon" was the name eventually adopted for this unique discovery.

The designer, Gabrielle (Coco) Chanel, used rayon during 1915 for a collection of model gowns but it was in the "under-world" that artificial silk really proved successful. A cheap, attractive substitute for the REAL THING — it meant that working class girls could indulge themselves in the sort of undies previously only bought and worn by the rich.

"Art Silk" had taken nearly thirty years of research to reach such popular acclaim; experiments had been tried as early as 1891. It was to be the first chapter in the story of man-made textiles.

Illustrated are two pairs of rayon directoire knickers of the late 1920s, early 1930s. Safely gathered at the knee with double elastic — one pair is bridal white and very shiny, the other, blush pink, sports a deep V front panel and appliqué flowers in the dull, reverse material.

Did you know corn protein could look like this?

"Art"
"Craft"
Rayon directoire
knickers
1920-30s

KNICKERS AT WAR

1939–1945: the years of the Second World War – bringing, as always during a war, endless restrictions and regulations to civilian life.

A Utility Scheme was introduced, and strict rationing of material became inevitable, and with it a stagnation of the fashion industry. Clothing coupons, the CC41, were issued, and three had to be surrendered to buy a pair of knickers.

Knitting was a very worthwhile and popular pastime during the war – all that time spent in air raid shelters needed some sort of portable hobby. All kinds of imaginable – or unimaginable – garments were knitted! Woolly knicks (1 coupon) and cami's (2) were among them.

Illustrated, are two articles of knitted undies reproduced from 1940s "Stitchcraft" patterns.

"Nylon" – the wonder fabric – was finally developed after eleven years of research by the American firm of Du Pont in 1938. This remarkable, entirely synthetic fibre was first used commercially to make stockings, and later underclothes. But between time, the war needed all the stocks of nylon that could be produced – for ropes, tents and parachutes. At a time of severe material shortage, the chance of laying your hands on a damaged parachute was treasure trove indeed. This would provide a whole family of girls with much-needed underwear – and, if necessary, a wedding dress!

These are a pair of knickers, wide cut with a side buttoning, made in the 1940s as part of a wedding trousseau. They are most beautifully handsewn – the needlework so precise that it looks like a machine.

Blue woollen cami knickers and 'shorts'.
both hand knitted
early 1940's
Black cotton lace cami knickers
Parachute nylon French knickers

They were made from the gleanings of a nylon parachute — often called "parachute silk".

The only disadvantage of wearing this close, fine quality nylon was the heat — you simply melted inside it . . .

1945 black cotton lace Camiknickers:

Very feminine and romantic. Homemade. "Well, I had to do something," said the woman who gave them to me, "It was the end of the war — you couldn't buy anything pretty — and I hadn't seen my husband for several years . . . " I have a vivid memory of this charming lady, a long-standing member of the Mothers' Union, arriving at my front door proffering these "Come hither" cami's with one hand — and a bag of frozen raspberries with the other. Bless her heart!

THE HAPPIEST DAYS OF YOUR LIFE?
A LASTING IMPRESSION.

A woman who was at school in the late 1920s reveals that she wore . . .
"Large knickers made of denim which were thick and hot, with elastic so tight I thought I would be permanently scarred, under which were worn white liners, equally hot. We changed the blue ones every THREE weeks and the white liners once a week . . ."

PURELY PERSONAL

Like the deep seated complaint voiced from above, I too, as a schoolgirl of the early 1950s, can only echo a strong fellow feeling.

My school knickers were fleecy-lined, bottle-green yarn and, again, cotton liners were always worn. The greatest discomfort came from the heat — they were terrifically hot to wear. They were also very ugly and essentially unfeminine — we went through agonies if a "boy" came, perchance, within our vicinity.

Even at the age of thirteen, I was struck by the sheer unattractiveness of "growing girls" prepared for games or "gym", clad in Aertex shirts and these horrible green bloomers. The gap between the tight leg-elastic bottom and the knee-sock top being an area of colour change according to the season — thus, blue in winter and bright pink in summer.

As I bear the name of woman — I record that there have been no sad songs sung over the passing of these vile coverings.

Strangely enough, having said that — I was then forced to admit that as a dress historian I would very much liked to have had an example of these school horrors in the Collection . . . but, search as I might, I could not unearth a single pair of the ghastly things. I concluded that they had all been burnt at the stake or dropped, at the dead of night, down a deep, dark pit — never to be seen again. Imagine my surprise, and collector's delight, when a whole boxful was sent to me, all beautifully packaged and catalogued . . . and to find that my generous donor was a gentleman!

I can never thank him enough; he supplied, in navy-blue, bottle-green, maroon, scarlet, greyest grey and darkest brown, the missing links in this story.

Just holding a pair of bottle-greens brought tears to my eyes!

Dating from the 1940s and 1950s the manu- facturers' labels read like a Roll of Honour; Montfort, Woollaton, Alpine Interlock, Bairnswear, Three Swans (more like Ugly Ducklings) Qualesta and — quite splendid — Puritex Hygienic (surely Headmistress Approved?)

Ah! Is all forgot??

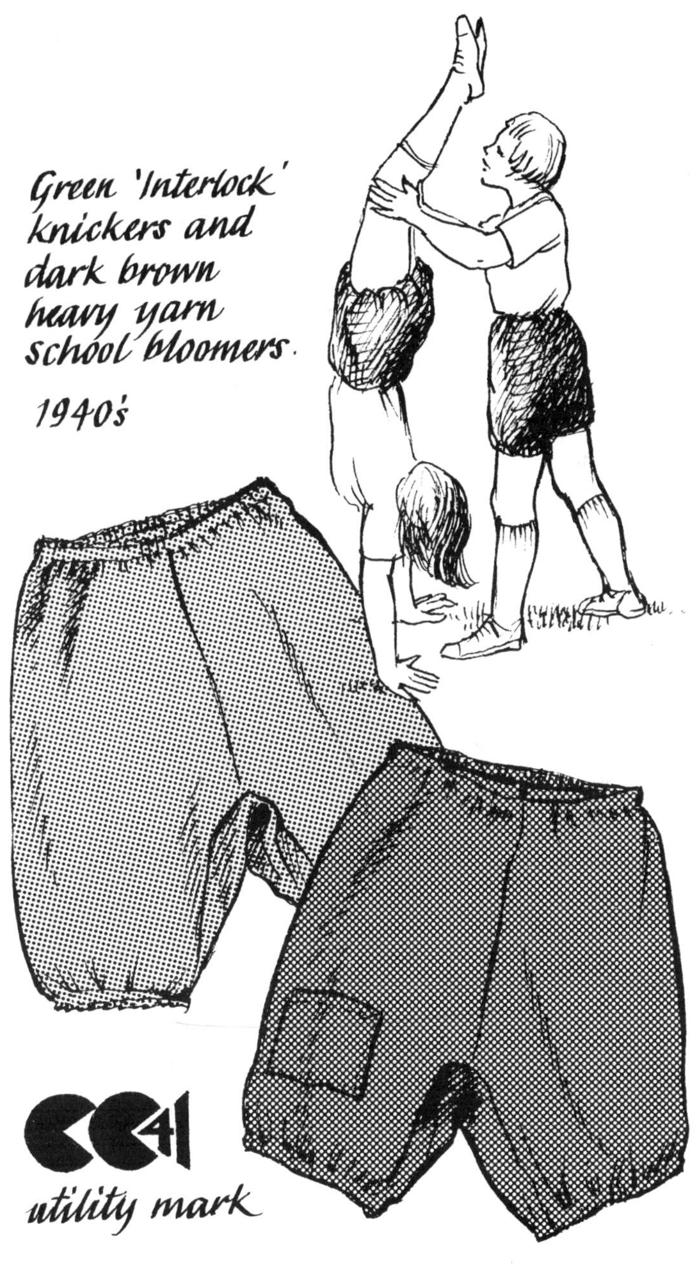

Green 'Interlock'
knickers and
dark brown
heavy yarn
school bloomers.
1940's

CC41
utility mark

HURRAH FOR HOT AND STICKY SCHOOLGIRLS

Advertisement from a 1937 Daniel Neal catalogue:

"The New School Knicker"
Lastex Yarn in Waist and Legs

The enormous demand we have received for this new knicker is indicative of its success and popularity among schools. It has several special features which appeal strongly to all who regard health with the importance it deserves. Instead of the usual elastic which frequently nips and interferes with healthy circulation, we have had a wide band of Lastex yarn knitted into the waist and legs. This clings in a most determined fashion, but without the slightest constriction or pressure. In between the legs, where so much wear comes, there is an extra large double gusset. Woven from a two-fold Botany yarn in navy, cream, brown, fawn and green.
Sizes 2 − 8
Ages 4 − 17
Retail prices 4/9 − 7/-
"The Knicker Lining"
A knicker lining in hygienic cellular fabric with trunk legs and Lastex waist-band. Designed specially to wear under the above knickers. Easily washed and most comfortable in wear. In cream only.
All sizes
Retail price 2/6

THE STUFF THAT DREAMS ARE MADE OF...

Women in uniform — Service Dress, in the first years of the Second World War — wore directoire knickers, in drear uniform colours, khaki, navy, black, blue/grey. The directoire style was considered necessary under their rapidly shortening skirts (which were thought practical and used less material). The advised skirt length was to the knee by 1941.

These unflattering knickers were dubbed "Passion Killers" . . . and the name stuck.

Here are three examples of slaughtered emotions. Not that any of these saw much in the way of Active Service (at least I don't think so!). Sadly I have no Service Dress examples in the Collection — I have a feeling that those that did not get worn out were burned on a bonfire and "Good Riddance" chanted over them.

A pair of black "Celanese" (trade name of The British Celanese Company Limited) knickers, c.1939. Machine embroidered rayon, blue forget-me-nots (as if one would, in these?) on a pale pink ground, c.1940.

Lobster pink "slipper" satin, machine stitched — the sort of hideous garment that I was still being taught to make at school in the early 1950s.

An ex-Wren friend tells me that their navy blue issue directoire knickers were called "Blackouts". They were absolutely detested and generally never worn. They were kept purely for display at female "kit muster" inspections to show that they were part of the regulation uniform. The only time she remembers wearing them was for the annual medical check-up when it was a "knickers-only-under-a-dressing-gown" order!

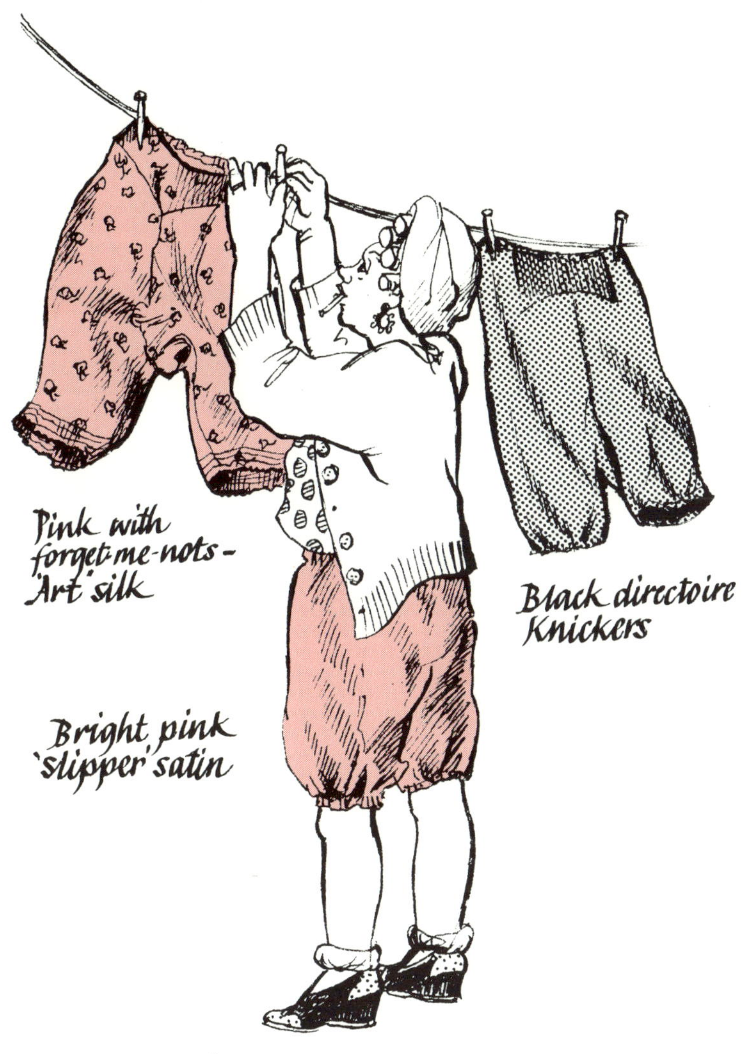

"Passion-Killer" c.1940

NEW LOOK NYLON

The French master of fashion, Christian Dior, launched his famous "New Look" in 1947. He created a pleasingly curved, cinch-waisted woman who wore long, full skirts and frothy underwear. He produced an essentially elegant, happily feminine counterpart to the short-skirted, square-shouldered, sensibly-tweeded, hand-knitted creature who had been masquerading as a woman since the beginning of the war.

I cannot imagine that '"The Master" ever allowed or tolerated his impeccably groomed beauties to wear woolly knickers!

So the nylon explosion began. Women demanded full, wide petticoats to go under their full, wide skirts — the crinoline was big business once again. The 1950s was a runaway decade for the nylon textile industry. The patent had been granted to the British Nylon Spinners in 1939, and Bri-nylon became a famous brand name of the 1950s.

Knickers — now often called "briefs", for such they had become — came in every conceivable pastel shade, complete with nylon frills. The counters of High Street clothes shops foamed with layers of drip-dry nylon underwear.

The only problem with this wonderful, easily-washed nylon finery was that the frills had a tendency to peel off — often with embarrassing results . . . remembering a girl-friend wearing a very wide, light skirt in the mid-1950s, who caught her knicker frill on the edge of a bus seat one hot summer's day — and, blissfully unaware, was half way off the bus before she realised that she was still attached!

St Michael
REGD
Nylon Lingerie
A selection of 1950's nylon knickers and briefs.

LACE DOUBLES

Gussie Moran, a handsome, blonde American girl took Wimbledon by storm in the summer of 1949. It was the result of some stylish tennis — she reached the Ladies' Doubles final — and eye-catching panties.

"Gorgeous Gussie", as she was affectionately nick-named, made the season of pedigree lawn tennis really hot stuff by wearing a pair of frilly lace panties, designed by Teddy Tinling, that were meant to be seen — much to the delight and appreciation of the spectators — and news journalists.

This was a shot in the right direction. When the peerless All England Croquet and Lawn Tennis Club was formed in 1877 — the lady members, bless them, played "polite", garden party tennis. The first — serious — Ladies' Championship was played in 1884 and the competitors wore long white flannel skirts, stiff-collared shirts, tight belts, petticoats, bustles, corsets, straw hats — and, certainly, well-hidden drawers.

Suzanne Lenglen was thought quite shocking in 1920 when she appeared in a simple, pleated, knee-length dress — albeit with firmly gartered white stockings. Helen Jacobs was the first woman to wear shorts at Wimbledon in the mid 1930s.

So, Gussie Moran, slamming her ball across the net of Tasteful Wimbledonia, provided the next positive, sartorial peak. Sssh . . . she brought sex-appeal to Centre Court — and was loved for it.

She may not be remembered for her tennis — but, all over the world "Gussie's" will always ring a bell!

"They're gorgeous, Gussie!"

THERE IS NOTHING LIKE A
DAME . . . UNDERNEATH

An early Christian martyr — Saint Pantaleone — has been immortalised for posterity by giving his name, via a complicated series of changes, to the very seat of modern life — in short, pants!

It so happened that in the great Italian Renaissance comedy of the sixteenth century, the Venetian character of "Pantalone" was an old, feeble man who wore tight-fitting trousers as part of his costume. He was one of the stock comic actors in any show.

He became adopted as one of the characters in Victorian pantomime — but by now he was a real clown in breeches — like Joseph Grimaldi. It was not until the early 1890s that Dan Leno, the famous comic, dressed himself up as a woman to play panto — and from that moment the "Dame" emerged as the chief comic role. The Dame has always, by tradition, had a scene where she undresses in front of the audience — and the big laugh has always been where she drops her drawers — or bloomers. The joke is that she wears more than one pair — each one more absurd, hilarious, and smaller, than the last.

Thus, there is usually a vast "patriotic" pair, a "topical/political joke" pair.

All leading up to the scandalous pair — and a blackout!

Old Mother England has had ...

she now...

grapples with...

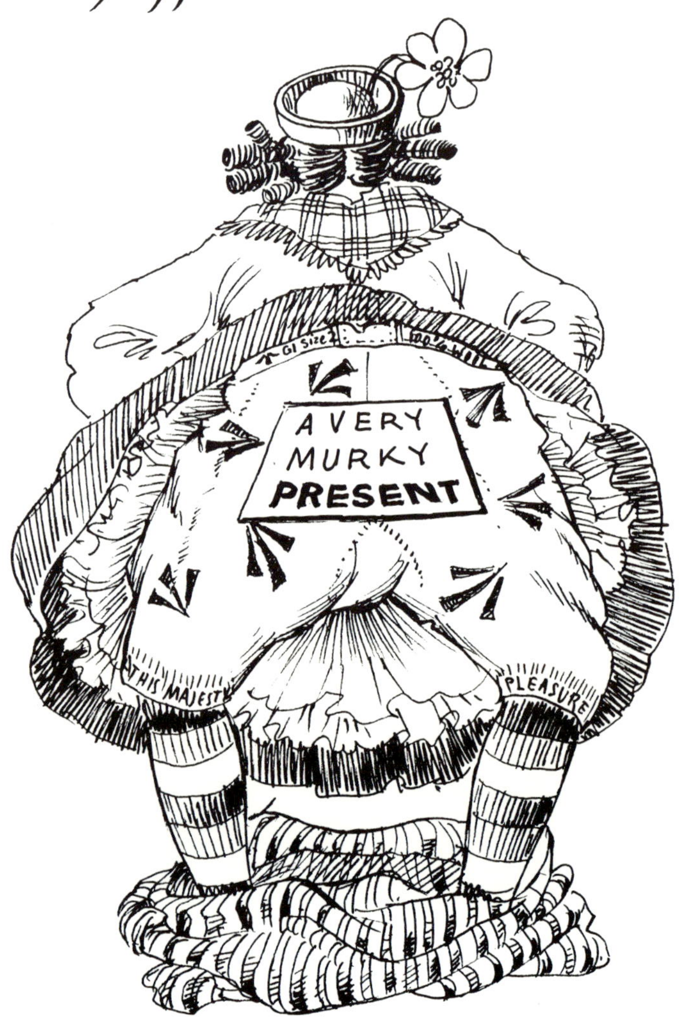

but, believe me, Lads...

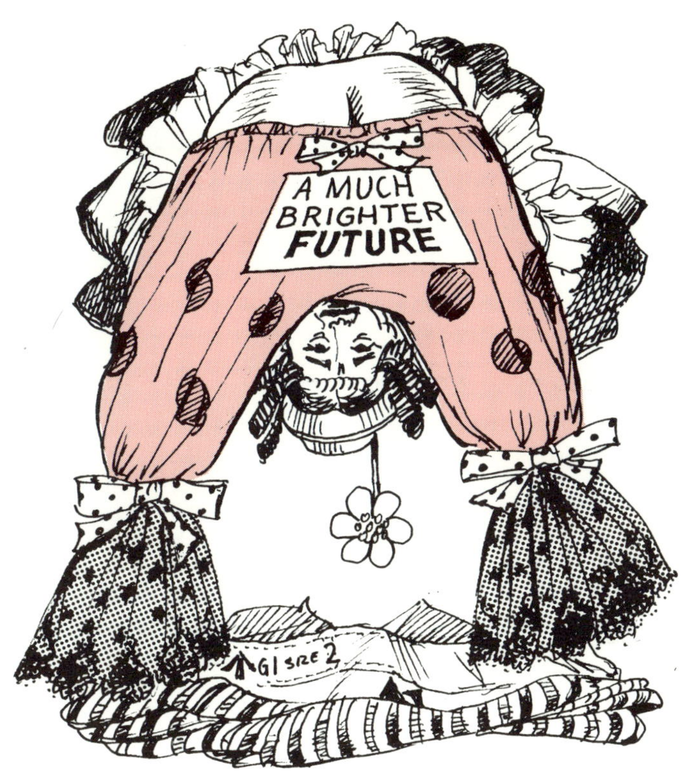

"They crowned me Queen of the May, m'dears
In 1893.
Because of the amenities of my anatomy.
They chased me 'ere and they chased me there . . .
And I didn't know what to do —
Oh it's dancin' in rivers that does the trick
And dabblin' in the dew!"
(Traditional Dame's Song)

BRING ON THE DANCING GIRLS . . .

The chorus girl has long been associated with frilly knickers — worn to show off the glamorous, high-kicking legs . . . from the mesmerising Moulin Rouge cancan dancers of the late nineteenth century who revealed the first really "French" knickers — swirling erotic white underwear contrasted against the black silk stockings and scarlet flounces of their dresses — to the modern, equally famous Las Vegas showgirl, who wears a rhinestone G-string and a handful of feathers.

These are two pairs of 1930s dance knickers that belonged to London chorus girls . . . cotton-lined, professionally cut and very strongly sewn, they have side and back openings with sets of extremely large and practical hooks and eyes for fastening. They are robustly made to withstand the rigours of dance routines — and quick changes. The name of the girl and the dance number is marked on each lining.

'Latin' dance
knickers and
separate frilled
'legs.'
c. 1938

LOTTIE'S LAMENT

"Lottie Collins lost her drawers
Will you kindly lend her yours?"

A Victorian couplet relating to Charlotte Collins, the London born Music Hall star who made famous the song "Ta-Ra-Ra-Boom-De-Ay".
In the 1890s Miss Collins would perform a frenzied, abandoned dance during her act — often leaving her faint with exhaustion in the wings (and legs!) — and, as my grandmother remembered, this ditty was the result.

I certainly first heard it as a small child spoken by my grandmother as she endeavoured to dress me on a cold winter's morning.

Lottie Collins
1890's

THE YEARS LAID WASTE . . .

The 1960s developed the nylon polyester textiles with ever-increasing rapidity — new "types" of nylon were added to the growing list of yarns. The outer clothes of this decade, at the end of which man reached the moon, were shorter and increasingly functional. Trousers and jeans became consistently worn by both sexes, and the mini-skirt was at its briefest in the late 1960s and early 1970s.

The clothes needed sleek, small, figure-hugging undies: the "bikini" style pants became popular in stretch nylon yarn. With the shortened skirts had come the advent of "tights" or "pantihose" as it is called in America.

Colours were "hot" — strong patterns were favoured: lime greens, pink, purple and orange, all seen blazing together — but a lot of women still preferred the traditional white underclothes.

Paper pants were first manufactured during the late 1960s — the first disposable undergarments. We have rapidly become the most wasteful, profligate society of any generation. Keeping clothes — of any sort — but most of all underclothes, is not considered necessary, or desirable.

As the tempo of life increased, women wanted polyester, Banlon, Lycra yarn — anything that could be chucked into a washing machine and forgotten — and eventually thrown out with the rubbish. The "Wear today — Trash tomorrow" society had taken only thirty years to establish. "Knickers in a twist" is an appropriate catch phrase and it neatly reflects the frenetic, ridiculous pace that society forces upon itself.

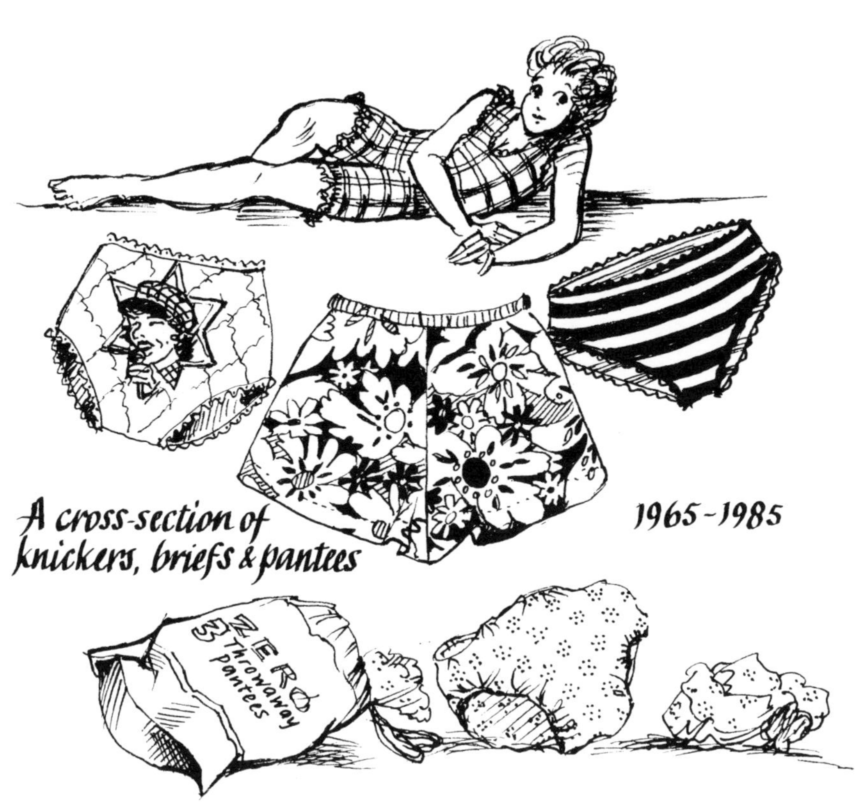
A cross-section of
knickers, briefs & pantees
1965-1985
ZERO
3 Throwaway
Pantees

Any collector of dress history would tell you that it gets harder each year to find examples of underwear of the last three decades. This particularly applies to knickers — which are continually replaced. Such humble clothes are not acceptable at jumble sales, and they make rotten dusters!

Only the elegant and exceedingly costly underclothes, by such enterprising designers as Janet Reger, will be the heirlooms of future generations. Sensuous silk and satin garments — recreating the fashions of the 1920s and 1930s are to the credit of Miss Reger, who so deftly and cleverly marketed them during the 1970s and 1980s. She succeeded in luring women — and thereby their men — back into the snare of romantic undies. Following suit, the big High Street shops now stock a wide range of cheaper pulse-racing, underclothes including camis — and French knickers.

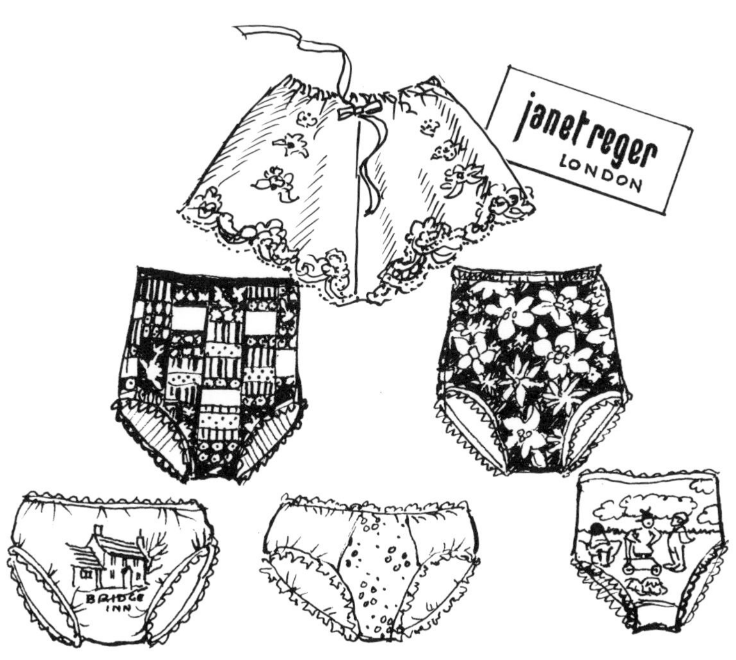

janet reger
LONDON
BRIDGE
INN

PATRIOTIC PAIR

Let's turn the tele on, dear,
Have the organ for a spell —
She's just arrived outside St. Paul's —
Oh, isn't she a belle!
What a superduper dress!
(Pity it's got crushed . . .)
But I expect with all the Hair-Do
She's been a little rushed.

DON'T twiddle with the knobs, dear,
It's perfect as it is —
Aren't her bridesmaids pretty?
Some of Her Lot — some of His.
Much nicer watching it at home;
It's better on the Box . . .
Look at all those diamonds?
To think they're real, not mocks!

D'you think Barbara Cartland's watching Her,
Like us, dear, on TV?
I think it's sad she didn't come —
All pearls and pink pongee.
Doesn't He look smart, dear?
But nervous though, I'm thinking . . .
Like you, dear, do you remember?
Pass the crisps, will you — I'm sinking.

Well, that's over! Pour some gin, dear,
Let's toast the Bride and Groom!
(I want to show you something
Now your mother's out the room)
What do you think of these, dear,
For the party at "The Stag"?
Souvenir of Charles and Di —
And how WE showed the flag!

These souvenir panties were worn to a ''Bad Taste'' party on Royal Wedding Night . . .

"EAST, WEST, WOOL IS BEST"

The Siberian wind blows the snows across our shores — and the need for wool is once again felt. Practical, comfortable, warm as toast undies have been making a quiet but positive "fashion" comeback (for some of us, such obviously sensible garments have NEVER gone out of fashion!)

Ladies' woollen underclothes have been made by famous firms like Wolsey and John Smedley Limited for almost a century — before that they had made hosiery and, of course, gentlemen's underwear.

Currently, "thermal" is the word that denotes keeping Jack Frost from biting at the nether regions. "Thermal" is a manufacturing process whereby the air is trapped in small "cells" or "pockets" — this holds the body's own heat between the material and the skin. Very simple, very scientific. Damart, an underwear chainstore that specialises in winter warmers, has developed thermolactyl — a blend of synthetic and natural fibres. Wolsey still do a large percentage of their products in pure wool — and, for real luxury, cashmere.

Combinations are rarely worn nowadays, but Marks & Spencer has a range of feminised longjohns in red, black and white, and lavender.

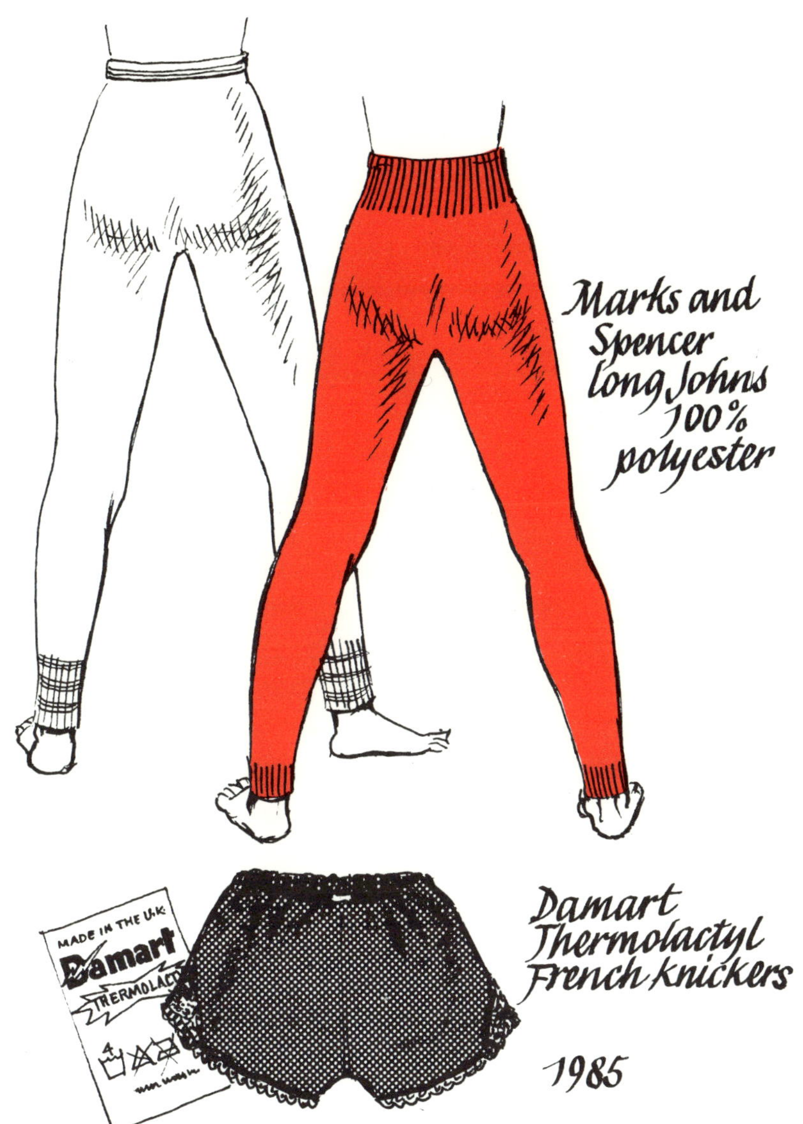

Marks and
Spencer
long Johns
100%
polyester

Damart
Thermolactyl
French knickers

1985

MADE IN THE U.K.
Damart
THERMOLACTYL

BRING OUT THE BEAST IN ME . . .

Three pairs of so-called "naughty knickers". Titillating wisps of metallic nylon lace, black Lycra and a silver tassel. The thrill-in-a-minute undies that, we are told, men love to buy women. The provocative bits of nonsense that create the illusion of wanton lustfulness.

I was told, sadly, by a proprietor of a "Naughty Knicker" shop that the saucy garments are often returned by the lady in question and exchanged for something . . .

. . . less saucy!

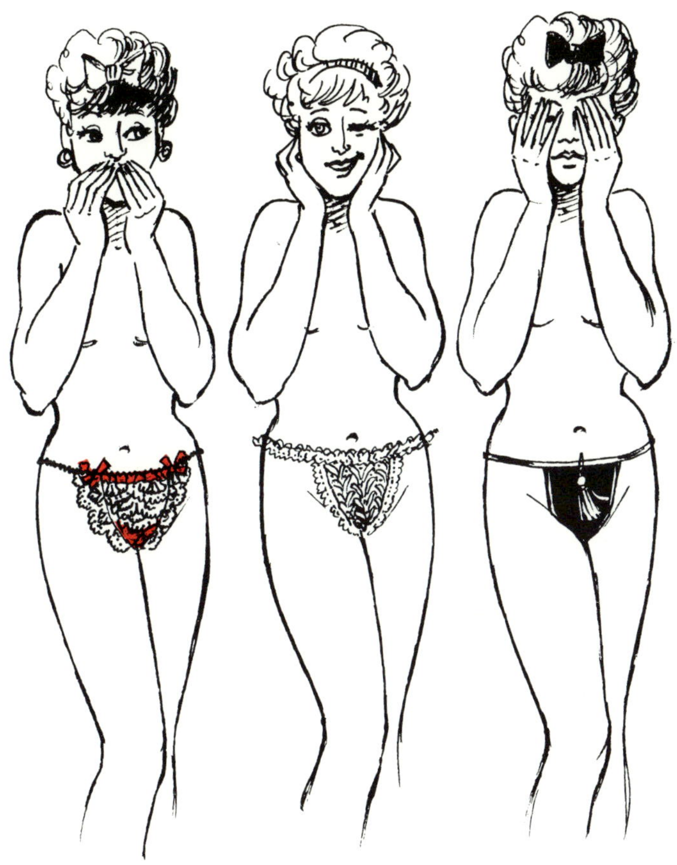

'Air on a G-String'

THE LEGEND OF THE LOST ELASTICS . . .

There are a wealth of stories — all of them true, I'm certain — concerning downsliding knickers. For example:

Some years ago, a doughty matron of considerable age and respectability was trying to cross the High Street of a country town to join her relatives in a hotel on the opposite side. It so happened that the street was closed to traffic, as a royal visit was about to take place, and the pavements were crowded. A policeman cautioned the lady not to cross as the procession was due any moment — she insisted she must, and he relented but told her to hurry. She proceeded to cross the road, but halfway across found her movements strangely hampered, her knickers having descended to her ankles. With the greatest presence in mind, she stood still, stepped out of them and, picking them up, waved them with a flourish to the crowds — and received cheers and an enormous burst of applause! She then escaped into the hotel seconds only before the royal motor car appeared.

It is early 1945; "doodlebugs" growling overhead. The place, Hythe, in Kent. A little girl of eight years old is playing in her garden. The "doodlebugs" are being shot down and exploding at regular intervals (amazing how children will play under any conditions!). Shirley has been forbidden to leave the garden by her mother. She gets bored and goes along to a friend's house. A "doodlebug" lands in Shirley's garden — her mother hysterical! Shirley returns innocently, one knickerleg hanging below her knee, the elastic having "gone". Mother, in relief,

KINGS ARMS

picks on this as a release from her anguish and Shirley is indignant: she denies drooping knickers as having been her fault and says, with great dignity, "It must have been the *blast*, Mummy!"

I am told on certain authority that many, many older women still like to put a safety pin into their waist knicker-elastic before venturing out . . . better, by far, to be safe . . . than embarrassed!

Early drawers were a novelty and it seems they were often made with the legs imperfectly attached to each other. From an unsigned letter dated 1820, the lady complains that:

"They are the ugliest things I ever saw; I will never put them on again. I dragged my dress in the dirt for fear someone would spy them; the brown and blue checked gingham I had in the house. My first dimity pair with real Swiss lace is quite useless to me for I lost one leg and did not deem it proper to pick it up, and so walked off leaving it in the street behind me, and the lace had cost six shillings a yard. I saw that mean Mrs. Spring wearing it last week as a tucker. I told her that it was mine and showed her the mate, but she said she hemmed and made it herself — the bold thing.

I hope there will be a short wearing of these horrid pantalets, they are too trying."

. . . FOR SHAME

The favourite horror story: generations of mothers who urge their daughters to be sure to have on clean, respectable knickers — in case they are knocked over by a bus and carted off to hospital!

VICTORIAN WASHING HINTS

Washing made easy: one of the best bleaching and emollient agents in washing person or clothing is borax. Dissolve in hot water, ¾ lb to the 10 gallons; a great saving in soap is effected by its use. It will not injure the most delicate fabric; laces and other fine tissues may be washed in a solution of borax with advantage to colour.

Washing, Ready and Effective mode of: dissolve 1lb of soap in 3 quarts of boiling water, the night before washing. Beginning to wash, put the soap into the dolly tub, add 8 tablespoonfuls of spirit of turpentine, and 6 ditto of hartshorn. Pour upon the above 8 gallons of boiling water. Have the clothes ready assorted; begin with the fine ones. Dolly each lot about five minutes, wash them in hot water in another dolly-tub, if you have it, next in blue water. When the water is getting cool, put it into the boiler to boil kitchen towels and other greasy things.

N.B. The quicker the washing is done, the better. As soon as one lot is taken out of the dolly-tub put another one in whilst the others are being rinsed. A little pipe-clay dissolved in the water employed in washing linen cleans the dirtiest linen entirely, with about one half the labour, and saving full one half of soap. Blueing: The blue bag is used for white articles. It helps to make them a better colour, and prevents them from going yellow. A few drops of ammonia added to the blue water helps to make them even whiter.

Lace: white lace should be washed with white soap in fairly hot water. Change the water frequently, and add soap to all as lace does not need rinsing. Pin to dry on a board covered with a linen cloth. Fine lace is never ironed. To colour lace after washing, put into warm water to which sufficient made coffee has been added to colour the lace (straining the coffee first through double muslin). Honiton lace should be folded evenly together and tacked lightly in a piece of flannel. Double the flannel over it and squeeze constantly. Never use hot water. Pull into position and leave to dry down. Do not iron.

Starching: boiling water starch is made in the following way: one tablespoonful of starch, three tablespoonfuls of cold water, half a teaspoonful of borax and a small piece of white wax. Mix the ingredients to a smooth paste, pour on about a quart of boiling water, stirring all the time until smooth, and add a pint of cold water. The starch is now ready for use. If one teaspoonful of sugar is added, the articles will be more glossy when ironed and retain their stiffness longer. To prevent starched articles from sticking to the iron, add a little alum to the starch before pouring the boiling water on. To stiffen lace, use cornflour instead of starch, as this will make it firm, yet not stiff; never starch fine lace.

'Dolly' and tub

THE WAY OF THE WORLD

Finally, in 1984, Calvin Klein made it fairly plain, in this sharing, liberated society, that the end was in sight. He launched a range of knickers designed for men — with women in mind.

So — what's half a knicker between friends?

But what our mid-Victorian great-grandmammas would have thought, I shudder to think.

IN MEMORIAM . . .

Extracts from letters I have been sent while writing this book.

From a lady in Southampton:
" . . . I feel I must tell you of my great-grandmother's drawers. They consisted of two separate legs attached to a waistband and overlapping at the waistband, so no crotch covering. They were made of a calico-like material, with embroidery at the knee edge — and now the crunch! — they were *starched* and also 'blue-ed' — thus pale blue knickers by a blue rinse — not white as the material would have been when purchased. My great grandmother died in 1939 aged 94 . . . " (So born in 1845)

From a gentleman in Sandwich, Kent:
" . . . I can remember as a small boy that my mother used to wear most elaborate knickers and I used to be most intrigued when I saw them hanging on the washing line. They were of linen and started at her waist — where they were held not by elastic but by buttons and they reached down to just below her knees where they ended in two frills of lace. They had a buttoned-up flap at the back and a slit up the front. They must have taken quite a lot of making and I believe she used to make her own. I can remember lots of sewing going on in the evenings . . . "

This is the stuff that real history is made from.

"Red hat — No drawers" goes the old saying; and,
who knows . . .

        . . . it may be right at that . . .

ACKNOWLEDGEMENTS

Rosemary Hawthorne wishes to thank:

Dr. C., dearest of friends, who in the interest of research risked both his reputation and the wrath of the B.M.A.!
Margaret Bond, for her valuable information and memories reaching back to the 1890s;
Molly Griffin, for her perfect laundering;
Margaret Smith, fellow collector, for sharing her knickers (see-mores; Prue's unbelievables);
Shirley Puckett for her stories and enthusiasm for this project;
Anne Sinstadt, for her research and trail-blazing on 'Knickers';
Olive Webb, for knitting up the 1940s patterns;
Ted Gilliver, artist and builder, for publicity photographs;
Janet Burnett, for deciphering my handwriting and typing the original manuscript;
The John Lewis Partnership archive collection for permission to quote from a Daniel Neal advertisement.
Curtis Brown Ltd for extract from *Great Days and Jolly Days* copyright Celia Haddon.
But, most of all, the numerous Ladies — and Gentlemen — wishing to remain anonymous, who have diligently searched out, hunted and retrieved knickers from every far-flung corner, so that I could complete this work.

"It's all in the interest of research, Madam"

BIBLIOGRAPHY

The History of Underclothes — C. Willett
    Cunnington and Phillis Cunnington
The Perfect Lady — C. Willett Cunnington
The Handbook of English Costume — C. Willett
    Cunnington and Phillis Cunnington
The Encyclopaedia of World Costume —
    Doreen Yarwood
The Habits of Good Society — By a gentleman
    and matron of Society
Enquire Within — 19th century
The Lady's Newspaper — 1848
The Guinness Guide to Feminine Achievements
Great Days and Jolly Days — Celia Haddon
Fashion in Underwear — Elizabeth Ewing
Dress and Undress — Elizabeth Ewing
Everyday Dress 1650–1900 — Elizabeth Ewing

The examples used in this book are part of the
Rosemary Hawthorne Collection.

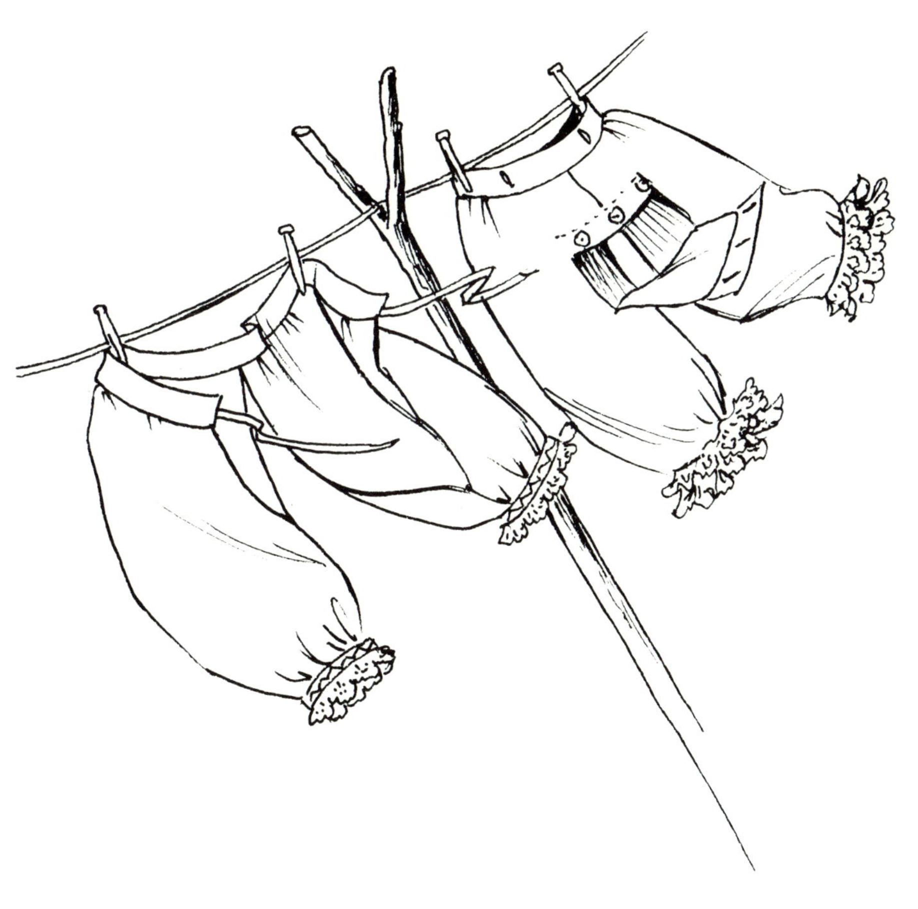

'Bosom friends' – an uplifting history!

As a natural sequel to Oh...Knickers Mary Want and I move up-market for the next book. Corsets and bras are the target and what a fascinating history they make! The ins and outs of tight-lacing over several hundred years right up to the 'No-bra' brigade, make breathtaking description and drawing.

If you think Oh...Knickers has broadened your education, then, dear reader, Bosom friends will widen it further ...